2004 POE

ONC
A RHYME

IMAGINATION FOR
A NEW GENERATION

Poems From The East
& East Midlands
Edited by Steve Twelvetree

First published in Great Britain in 2005 by:
Young Writers
Remus House
Coltsfoot Drive
Peterborough
PE2 9JX
Telephone: 01733 890066
Website: www.youngwriters.co.uk

SB ISBN 1 84460 650 3

Foreword

Young Writers was established in 1991 and has been passionately devoted to the promotion of reading and writing in children and young adults ever since. The quest continues today. Young Writers remains as committed to engendering the fostering of burgeoning poetic and literary talent as ever.

This year's Young Writers competition has proven as vibrant and dynamic as ever and we are delighted to present a showcase of the best poetry from across the UK. Each poem has been carefully selected from a wealth of *Once Upon A Rhyme* entries before ultimately being published in this, our twelfth primary school poetry series.

Once again, we have been supremely impressed by the overall high quality of the entries we have received. The imagination, energy and creativity which has gone into each young writer's entry made choosing the best poems a challenging and often difficult but ultimately hugely rewarding task - the general high standard of the work submitted amply vindicating this opportunity to bring their poetry to a larger appreciative audience.

We sincerely hope you are pleased with our final selection and that you will enjoy *Once Upon A Rhyme Poems From The East & East Midlands* for many years to come.

Contents

Alison Jarvis (8)   32
Benita Mercedes Leone (8)   33
Rebecca Wilkins (8)   34
Katie Osborne (7)   35
George Coates (8)   36
Joshua Harris (8)   37
Esther Lucy Harris (8)   38
Scott Hamilton (8)   39
Molly Kendall (8)   40
Isabel Hutchings (7)   41

Chalkwell Hall Junior School, Leigh-on-Sea
Barney Snoxell (8)   42

Cringleford VA CE First & Middle School, Norwich
Anna Hoogkamer (9)   43
Megan Grainger (9)   44
Jessica Grace Bird (9)   45
Pollyanna Payne (9)   46
Ellie Davies (9)   47
Alice Mary Smith (10)   48
Eleanor Girling (10)   49
William Capon (9)   50
Samuel Cane (9)   51
Jack Latoy (9)   52
Sydney Laing (9)   53
William Spalding   54
William Calder (10)   55
Naomi Grant (9)   56
Georgina Page (9)   57
Sandy Ni'Man (9)   58
Scott McCrum (9)   59
Debbie Stapleford (9)   60
Laura Doswell (9)   61

Docking Primary School, Docking
Emily Able (9)   62
Nikki Brennan (10)   63
Liam Craig (10)   64
Alice Dean (9)   65

Lake View Primary School, Mansfield

Our Lady Of Lourdes RC Primary School, Leigh-on-Sea

St Augustine's Junior School, Worksop

Carrie-Ann Taylor (10)   100
Sarah Cliffe (10)   101

St Martin at Shouldham CE VA Primary School, King's Lynn
Kate Knowles (10)   102
Dale Bettridge (9)   103
Anna Blakie (10)   104
Oliver Ware (10)   105
Charlie Perkins (10)   106
George Chapman (10)   107
Rory Blake (9)   108
Liam Holbeche-Smith (9)   109
Oliver Johnson (9)   110
Katherine Blakie (10)   111
Lewis Findull (10)   112
Morgan Massurit (9)   113
Kayley Stabler (9)   114
Maisie Silverman (10)   115
Jasmine Haskett (10)   116
Daniella Bottone (9)   117
Calum Wilson (11)   118
Greg Mitchell (10)   119

Townley School, Christchurch
Ben Stanhope (11)   120
Aaron Whittaker (10)   121
Daniel Rushton (10)   122
Emily Chisholm (10)   123
Alex Andrews (10)   124
Ollie Haylock (10)   125
Steven Leeman (10)   126
Georgina Clifford (10)   127
Ryan Tominey (10)   128
Becca Jackson (10)   129
Ellie Jackson (10)   130
Damien Campbell Warby (10)   131
Chantelle Coxall (10)   132

Wheatfields Junior School, St Albans

Ernest Hill (10)	133
Tom Girdlestone (10)	134
Francesca Knight (9)	135
James Riding (8)	136
Raveena Virdee (10)	137
Lydia Spooner (9)	138
Brent McCormick (10)	139
Kate Upton (8)	140
Jack Caddy (9)	141
Richard Breislin (10)	142
Holly Winfield (8)	143
Paige Young (10)	144
Larissa Begg (8)	145
Jonathan Chambers (9)	146
Nicholas Gachowicz (11)	147
Joseph Crosby (8)	148

The Poems

Flying Books

Every night the moon's light
The books make a fight
You don't like scripe pipe
'Cause laser zaps my type
And that's why we fight.

One book flew away
And went for two days.
We hate each other
Shhh!
You're dead meat.

That's why we fight
That's why we fly at midnight.
When the other book came
It's made of shame
Why didn't you read me?

William Merrett (7)

The Ghost

When I was sleeping, a-sleeping,
I heard a creeping
In my corridor.

Then a tapping, a-tapping,
Maybe a rapping,
Upon my chamber door.

I then heard a creeping, a creeping
Maybe a squeaking,
Upon a floorboard.

Then a hazy figure appeared before me,
Soaked in blood, it was a ghastly thing to see.
When I saw it, I did flee.

Down the stairs I did run and hurry,
No time for fear, no time to worry.
Down the stairs and into the library.

Yet again the spirit did reappear,
This time it was very near
And very clear.

'What business hath you with me?' I said.
'What reason hath you to wake me from my bed?
The spirit raised its head and said:

'I am the ghost of Marc de Veer
Murdered was I, not far from here,
With an axe in my neck and my body in Bowman Mere.'

At that point the spirit grabbed his hair and pulled off his head,
Thrust it in the air and said . . .
I then fainted clean away and I woke up the very next day.
I travelled to Bowman Mere,
With a spade I dug and saw my fear,
- the body of Marc de Veer.'

Sandip Samanta (10)
Bancroft's Preparatory School, Woodford Green

Little Red Riding Hood

Poor old gran,
She's bunged up in bed.
I'll take her some wine,
And give her some bread.

I went down the road,
Wrapped in my cloak.
I reached her house,
Chimney a' smoke.

I banged on the door,
She answered my call.
There stood a figure,
(Gasp!) not Gran at all!

Great big eyes,
Great big ears,
Great big paws,
'I'll eat ya, me dears!'

I then tried to run,
But she ate me for tea.
The axe man came
And set me free.

Simon Russell (10)
Bancroft's Preparatory School, Woodford Green

A Set Of Limericks

There was a young girl from the Rockies,
Who thought she could beat all the jockeys.
She jumped on a horse
And galloped the course.
Wearing hard hat, breeches and sockies!

A bat in the London Tower
Slept there for many an hour.
But when she awake
She started to choke
That stuffy old bat in the Tower!

There was an old man from New Guinea,
Who spent all his life in a pinny,
When he got in his car,
To visit the bar,
His friends all laughed at him, 'Ninny!'

There was a young boy from Wales,
He owned a collection of snails.
They were large, they were small,
They stuck to the wall
And left slimy trails over Wales!

Linnet Kaymer (10)
Bancroft's Preparatory School, Woodford Green

A Rainy Day In London

(This poem was inspired by the picture of a rainy day in London)

The lemon-yellow sky
Stands out from everything in sight;
Umbrellas - sway in the breeze,
A blackbird takes flight
Horses' hooves
Pattering against slippery cobbles
People walking
Out of town
An old lady solemnly hobbles.
The sweet smell of bread
Floods the air,
The people's feet
Clatter and splatter
In the puddles, oh so deep.
They don't stop,
Whatever the matter.
A gentleman
Stands beside
A lady with golden earrings
That glimmer
In the morning sun.
Towering lamp posts shimmering
As I turn the corner,
The voices disappear,
The clattering of the horses fade
But the rain is here to stay.

Stephanie Posner (10)
Bancroft's Preparatory School, Woodford Green

Dino

Dino is my dog's name,
To him, life is just a game.
He's black and fluffy and very, very cute,
And he ate my dad's boot.
We play all day,
He only came in May.
He's just a little puppy
But my goodness he sure is mucky!

Xandria Levy (9)
Bourton Meadow School, Buckingham

All I Wanted Was A Friend

All I wanted was a friend to play with,
to be with,
So I got one when I went to school,
he always liked me
but now we have parted
I don't know why.
He doesn't talk to me much
he doesn't play with me much,
my blue eyes fill with tears.
Maybe it was something I did
I will never know,
I don't know what to do
invite him to my party?
But I've invited Glen
and I'm only allowed to take one.
My blue eyes fill with tears
maybe it was something I did -
I'll never know.

Jacob Barker (9)
Bourton Meadow School, Buckingham

Volcano

I see smoke coming out of the volcano,
It gets redder and redder.
The ground starts to shake,
Then it goes, bang, bang and bang!
Lava rolls down the mountain.
Volcano! Volcano! Volcano erupts!

David Ellis (9)
Bourton Meadow School, Buckingham

Football

Football is the game
You get lots of fame,
You try and score
Because the goalie might be poor.
You might be sheer class
Or you might be better blowing the brass.
You might win
Or get kicked in the shin
Or go in the sin-bin.

Daniel Staley (9)
Bourton Meadow School, Buckingham

I Do Have Feelings

I do have feelings
I do know what people say
I do like people, but maybe
Just maybe, people don't like me!
See, I do know and yes
I do have *feelings*.

Katie Harland (9)
Bourton Meadow School, Buckingham

Tiger Eyes

Tiger eyes, tiger eyes
prowling through the jungle,
Tiger eyes, tiger eyes
searching out his prey.
Tiger eyes, tiger eyes
proud, sleek and wild.

Tiger eyes, tiger eyes
camouflaged in the grass,
Fierce, proud and
wild tiger eyes.

Andrew Cheshire (9)
Bourton Meadow School, Buckingham

Roller Coaster

Round and round we go
on the roller coaster
We'll stop in a minute
but I'm feeling sloppy as dough!
Hold on . . .
I think I'm going to be . . . !

Ellen Whitbread (9)
Bourton Meadow School, Buckingham

The Solar System

Jupiter, Saturn
Are in the solar system
Pluto, Sun, Earth
It wouldn't be without it
There are some more planets too
In the Milky Way
there are always lots of stars
In the blackness - stars
Bright stars
Hot burning gas
Different planets
There are nine we are related to
Bright stars.

Jamie Pollard (9)
Bourton Meadow School, Buckingham

Dogs

I love dogs, they are great,
I have a dog
She's called Pip.
I love her very much,
Some people say that
Dogs are man's best friend.
That's not true - girls love dogs too!

Hannah Ingle (9)
Bourton Meadow School, Buckingham

Shiny, Sparkling, Starry Things

They're shiny, sparkling, starry things
They dance with joy
They're full of light and always bright.

They're shiny, sparkling, starry things,
They twirl around and skip,
They dance and prance all night long.

They're shiny, sparkling, starry things,
All night long they jump and leap,
They're full of life, until they're lit.

They're dead, dull, dark things,
Burned away to dust,
They no longer dance, only rust.

Eloise Medland (9)
Bourton Meadow School, Buckingham

My Family

My family is here at home,
My marvellous mum,
My dashing dad,
Adorable Aiden
Confident Callum
And my great
Guinea pigs
And of course there is
Me.

Rhiannon N Taylor (9)
Bourton Meadow School, Buckingham

Fireworks

The sparks in the sky are glittering,
Boom. Crackle, crackle.
People scream with laughter,
Sparklers are burning
While the bonfire burns.
Somebody says, 'What are those things?'
Somebody else says, 'They're fireworks.'

Jonathan McNally (9)
Bourton Meadow School, Buckingham

Pony, Pony

Pony, pony, beautiful pony
Fly me through the meadows
Fly me though the fields
Canter over a humungous hedge
Jump, jump, this is fun
Flying through the meadows
With the birds and buttercups.

Zoe Gambling (9)
Bourton Meadow School, Buckingham

Football

Football is fun football
I always score cos the goalie is poor
I play for a great team, we always win
The other team might get to see the sin bin
You might get kicked in the shin
You might get hurt
But always win!

Robert Bysouth (9)
Bourton Meadow School, Buckingham

Pets, Pets, Pets

'I don't want a gerbil
I don't want a rat
I want a dog.'

'No that won't do.'

'I want a spider
Yeah I want a spider.'

'Spiders are ugly,
Spiders are gross,
I don't want a spider in my house.'

'I'll have a puppy then.'

'No you won't.'

'But . . .'

Peter Glasgow (9)
Bourton Meadow School, Buckingham

Munch Muncher

Lettuce muncher
Crisp cruncher

Hard case
Fresh base

Tomato killer
Crunchie filler

Soft top
You buy it in a shop.

Sophie Lewis (10)
Bourton Meadow School, Buckingham

My Mum

My mum is kinda funky,
She dresses really cool.
She likes to have a lot of fun
And sometimes acts the fool!

Sometimes we go out for the day,
Doing girly things.
Curling our hair, painting our nails,
Trying on diamond rings!

Sometimes we just sit and chat,
When I'm feeling blue.
Having lots of cuddles,
Which cheers me up too!

My mum is one in a million,
She's my best friend.
I love her really, lots and lots,
And that will never end!

Georgina Butler (10)
Bourton Meadow School, Buckingham

Guess What?

Loves mud,
Sometimes pink,
Quite large,
Usually stink.
Big nose,
Curly tail,
Really lazy,
Not frail.
?

Grace Watts (10)
Bourton Meadow School, Buckingham

Poachers

Why do poachers kill animals
- not let them stay and blink?
Why do poachers kill animals
don't they ever stop to think?
Animals don't deserve this,
they deserve to roam freely,
It's such a shame for poachers,
they could be doing something else, really.
So why do poachers do this,
do they find it fun?
I don't think it's that great really
to be shooting animals with a gun.

Emily May (9)
Bourton Meadow School, Buckingham

Paige And The Puppies

Paige was made about puppies
She had fifty posters, a hundred books
On puppies
And was happy like this, until one day
She turned into a puppy
And was happier!

Laura Primiceri (9)
Bourton Meadow School, Buckingham

Puppies

You can see their cute little faces
You can always imagine them playing with laces
Or even them in suitcases.

Fluffy, adorable ears
Their animal friends are deer.
They're so cute you can even end up in tears.

They always laugh and play
Their birthdays might be in May
You would always have a nice day.

All puppies love food, especially buns
They would always have fun
One day I hope I will get one.

Leah Ballinger (9)
Bourton Meadow School, Buckingham

Guess Who?

No heart
Made-up parts
Ruined clothes
Still pose
Hand pegs
Stick legs
Hat wearer
Crow scarer
What am I?

Emma Jones (10)
Bourton Meadow School, Buckingham

That's What The Children Need

Good tuition
For fruition,
That's what the children need.

Love and caring
Time for sharing,
That's what the children need.

More food to eat
And clean water to drink,
And no more rags,
And old paper bags
Wrapped around their knees,
That's what the children need.

Closer doctors,
And night watchers,
To keep the children safe from harm.

Gentler weather
And shoes of leather,
To keep the cold out from their toes.

That's what the children need,
That's what the children need.
Let the children be free,
From work and
Let the children be free
From war and
Let the children be free
For all eternity.

Kerry Fox (10)
Bourton Meadow School, Buckingham

Harvest Time

We gather seeds and wheat every year,
It's so tiring we have to use a tractor and a combine harvester.
Crops grow with sun and rain
The leaves fall into the sunny green meadows
And the sheep jump and play.
The squirrels climb, play and eat nuts.

George Buksmann (7)
Bunny CE Primary School, Nottingham

Harvest

Going to church
We do a play
The vicar comes
We sing and pray

Oats, wheat and barley
Bread, carrots and sprouts.

Zak Wright-Horne (7)
Bunny CE Primary School, Nottingham

Autumn

Oats, hay and barley,
Leaves fall, plough
Seeds fall from the trees,
The seeds, berries or leaves
Floating in the sky.
Sow, treat,
Warm glow.

Marcus Naden (7)
Bunny CE Primary School, Nottingham

Harvest Is The Best

Harvest, seeds grow on the trees,
Harvest, trees sway in the breeze
Combine harvester rustles by
Then the corn flies in my eye.

Reaping through the golden meadows
Lying on the cool green grass
Smelling the summer flowers
As we pass away the hours
Harvest is the best.

Alison Jarvis (8)
Bunny CE Primary School, Nottingham

Harvest

We gather corn, wheat, oats and barley
And plenty more
Acorns fall down from the trees
Squirrels eat the nuts and it's night-time.

Benita Mercedes Leone (8)
Bunny CE Primary School, Nottingham

Harvest Time

Vegetables that we eat,
What a lovely tasty treat.
Oats, corn, barley, wheat
Birds are nesting in the heat.

Tractors in the golden meadow
Animals go to hibernate
Whilst the farmers throw seeds from a plate.

When the leaves come tumbling down
Red, gold, green and brown
Soon it will be time to say goodbye,
Harvest, harvest about to die.

Rebecca Wilkins (8)
Bunny CE Primary School, Nottingham

Harvest Goods

Harvest seeds, corn and wheat
Leaves fall, beetles crawl
Animals, nuts, acorns, huts.
We are thankful for plenty of food
But now we come to give some to you.
The seeds off the trees flow into the breeze,
The crops in the ground are worth one pound,
The squirrel gathers plenty of berries.
The combine harvester ploughs
The crops and the rain drops.

Katie Osborne (7)
Bunny CE Primary School, Nottingham

Harvest

Look at the squirrels
Gathering berries from the
Treetops of the tree.
Look at the leaves falling
From the trees
And the birds and
The combine harvester
Cutting the wheat.

George Coates (8)
Bunny CE Primary School, Nottingham

My Harvest Poem

Every year I pick ripe berries . . .
growing on the trees.
In the summer when they grow
they're waiting for the breeze.
Harvest, harvest is the best,
it is better than all the rest.
If you don't believe me you will soon see,
the crops, the fruit, the vegetables and
the combine harvester and the animals.

Joshua Harris (8)
Bunny CE Primary School, Nottingham

Harvest

Running in the golden corn,
Lying on the cool green grass.
Some vegetables people love to eat
So that's definitely what I'd call a treat.
The squirrels gather nuts and berries
In the meadows green.
The animals take shelter at night
And they wake up to the sunshine beam.

Esther Lucy Harris (8)
Bunny CE Primary School, Nottingham

Harvest

Seeds flying through the air,
Berries getting picked off bushes.
The autumn breeze moves the leaves.

Scott Hamilton (8)
Bunny CE Primary School, Nottingham

Harvest Time

Reaping through the golden meadows,
Looking at the rows and rows,
Watching the leaves all different colours,
Go rushing by, flying around and
Touching the ground.
Harvest means a lot to me
Because of the birds,
That sway about in the sky.
I go to collect crops and berries.

Molly Kendall (8)
Bunny CE Primary School, Nottingham

Harvest

Leaves fall
Leaves fall
Leaves on the ground.

Corn, corn
In the field
Wheat and barley
Can be found.

Combine harvester
Cutting up the food
For us.

Isabel Hutchings (7)
Bunny CE Primary School, Nottingham

School Poem

When I go to school I say
There's no place like school.
I've got a nice teacher who's called
Mrs Cable.
I like my friends but we do
have our moments.
As I said, there's no place
like school.
But sometimes . . .
I'm a very bad boy.

Barney Snoxell (8)
Chalkwell Hall Junior School, Leigh-on-Sea

The Marguerites

In full bloom were the marguerites
Spanish people through Spanish streets.

The orange walls of orange houses
Whilst the lazy lizard drowses.

In full bloom were the marguerites
Spanish people through Spanish streets.

A sea of trees that meet the eye
Vapour trails sweep through the sky.

In full bloom were the marguerites
Spanish people through Spanish streets.

A five minute walk to the beach
Down to the corner shop to buy a peach.

In full bloom were the marguerites
Spanish people through Spanish streets.

The fairy of the marguerites
Watches people pass in the streets

In full bloom were the marguerites
Spanish people through Spanish streets.

Anna Hoogkamer (9)
Cringleford VA CE First & Middle School, Norwich

Windy Day

It was windy yesterday
And it is today,
And the trees sway
Like yesterday.

It was sunny last week,
It was great fun,
I was the only one
Last week, under the sun.

The flowers were blooming last weekend,
But the winds have made them all bend.
It's a shame, all their legs have been broken
It happens when autumn's awoken.

Megan Grainger (9)
Cringleford VA CE First & Middle School, Norwich

Move Your Feet

```
      n            n            n
    a   c        a   c        a   c
D       e    D       e    D        e
```
Is what I love to do.
Tap . . . tap . . . tap . . .
With my tap shoe.
Le - ap, le - ap, le - ap,
In my leotard.

```
      n            n            n
    a   c        a   c        a   c
D       e    D       e    D        e
```
None of these are hard.
```
                 w   r
```
Plíe, pirouette and t   i   l
Watch me go, the dancing girl!
```
         s                 y
         t                 a
         e                 w
```
Palm-push,   p, lunge and s
Is my joy each Saturday.
```
            en
```
Back, b   d, s-p-l-i-t-s
And head to toe
Can't wait for my new dancing show!

Jessica Grace Bird (9)
Cringleford VA CE First & Middle School, Norwich

My Climbing Frame

Made of steel, dull and grey
fills your day with fun and play.
One day I'm a sailor's ship
sailing the seas with Pirate Pip.
Another day I'm a castle tall
wizards in my high stone wall.
Making potions and some spells
maybe sometime, one that smells
Oh, I like pretending games, they're fun!
For me, my friends, for everyone.

Pollyanna Payne (9)
Cringleford VA CE First & Middle School, Norwich

What Is Red?

Red is a wobbly jelly
Red is a jam tart,
Red is the colour of roses
To give to your sweetheart.

Red is an apple
All juicy and sweet,
Red is my skin
After a days sizzling heat.

Red is a ruby
Sparkling with shine,
My dad likes to drink
A glass of red wine.

Red is blood
Dripping from my hand,
Red is the uniform
Of a marching band.

Red means you must stop
At a traffic light,
Red is the colour of sky
And a shepherd's delight.

Red is the colour
For a protest,
Red is the colour
That I like the best.

Ellie Davies (9)
Cringleford VA CE First & Middle School, Norwich

My Birthday

A ll I can think about is being ten
L aughing with my best friends
I cing on my birthday cake
C andles lit up, all ten of them
E very candle blown out
S eeing happy faces.

S ad that it's soon going to be over
P resents from my family and friends
E xcited about everything
C ards for a daughter, a sister, a grandaughter
I magining what's inside the wrapping paper
A ll of this seems like a dream
L ucky that I have people who love me.

W hy does this birthday have to be over?
E veryone has had a good time
E verything seems as if it is floating away
K eeping all of these memories in my mind.

Alice Mary Smith (10)
Cringleford VA CE First & Middle School, Norwich

The Pixie

I see above the pixie's head
Beautiful roses, berries red,

And as the pixie sits by the stream
I see grasses, some purple, some green.

I see next to the pixie's shoe
Little insects, forget-me-not's blue.

And as the pixie sits by the stream,
I see grasses, some purple, some green.

So now the pixie starts to mellow
I see the sunset, orange and yellow.

Eleanor Girling (10)
Cringleford VA CE First & Middle School, Norwich

Holidays

I like to go on holiday with my dad and mum,
they make sure that I have fun.
What I like to do the best
is sit by the pool and have a rest.
If it's hot and there's no pool,
then I go in the sea to keep cool.

If we go to the beach I like to play with the sand,
I don't have to play on my own because Daddy gives me a hand.
I like to snorkel in the sea
and watch all of the fish swim by me.
When I'm sitting on the beach,
I can hear the seagulls screech.

Sometimes on holiday we visit a city,
but that requires a lot of money in the kitty.
The city is noisy with lots of cars,
and we like to stop at the restaurants and bars.
We often order chicken and chips
and after we've eaten, we lick our lips.

Holidays are busy with lots to do,
Mum and Dad think so too.
Sometimes I think the holiday that's best,
is to stay at home and have a rest.

William Capon (9)
Cringleford VA CE First & Middle School, Norwich

A Bout

S trapping Sam
A nnounced a wrestling match against
M el Gibson.
U ppercut from Sam
'E ek!' shrieks Mel
L eft hook follows into the nose.

'C or! what a lot of blood'
A rm lock crushes Gibson's spindly arms
'N ow who's a hero?' shouts Sam.

'Flipping Nora!
  I 've been beaten,'
G rowls Mel,
'H igh time I retired,'
  T riumphant Sam agrees!

Samuel Cane (9)
Cringleford VA CE First & Middle School, Norwich

Wendy House

Auntie Wendy bought a house
Which she thought very nice
But when we went to check it out
We found it full of mice

It was very titchy
With mould here and there
We looked in the kitchen cupboard
And found a mouldy pear

When we went upstairs
We found it even worse
There was a hole in the ceiling
Where a water pipe had burst

When we came downstairs
We all began to stare
At a pig who had wandered in
And was standing just there

A year later we went to look
And found it much the same . . .
Except the cat was fat on mice
And the pig had gone insane!

Jack Latoy (9)
Cringleford VA CE First & Middle School, Norwich

1,000 Birds

I was sitting outside at the time,
Looking up at the sky.
I saw a plane, I saw some birds,
Things that can fly.

When suddenly it happened,
I didn't know what to do.
1,000 birds filled the skies,
And one stole my shoe.

The birds were beautiful,
Robins, canaries too.
Tropical birds, normal birds
And all calling, 'Coo, coo.'

I'm not sure whether I dreamt it,
1,000 birds, yeah right!
But I haven't got my shoe back
And 1,000 birds call every night!

Sydney Laing (9)
Cringleford VA CE First & Middle School, Norwich

The Dragon

Hiding in mysterious shadows
lurking in the highest cave,
somewhere in the darkened forest
a dragon gnarls his prey.

Blood dribbles down his teeth
red eyes shine in the light of the moon
his scales are black, tail is green
it's the scariest dragon you have ever seen.

He has two sharp horns upon his head,
like hollow caves, his nostrils flair.
One small glance and you'll be dead,
fire and steam, so best beware.

William Spalding
Cringleford VA CE First & Middle School, Norwich

Through The Jungle

Through the jungle you may see
the humming bees and birds in the trees.
Through the jungle you may see
lions growling and tigers prowling.

Through the jungle you may see
birds flying and things dying.

But of all the things colourful and bright
you will rarely find anything not right.

William Calder (10)
Cringleford VA CE First & Middle School, Norwich

Romance

The sound of clinking glasses
The sight of fizzy drinks
The smell of cherry bakewell
The colour of passion, pink and ruby-red
The feel of the velvety skin of a dolphin
The taste of red grapes
The flower of rose
The jewel of ruby.

Wonderful thing, isn't it?
Romance.

Naomi Grant (9)
Cringleford VA CE First & Middle School, Norwich

Dolphins

Have you seen a dolphin splashing in the sea?
Because if you haven't please come along with me.

Have you seen the way the sea splashes over me?
It comes right up and over my knee.

Have you seen the way the sun shines on the sea
While making rainbow colours that shine over me?

Have you seen the way the dolphin jumps so high?
It really does amaze me - he doesn't touch the sky.

Georgina Page (9)
Cringleford VA CE First & Middle School, Norwich

Yeah!

To imagine there are no aliens is very hard.
You'll understand what I mean
After I tell you about their landing
In my backyard.

The boy from next door
Was a witness to the scene,
When three of the aliens came out
Of a big bean!

They all headed towards the washing line,
I was very pleased, as it was mostly mine.

Old socks with some funny underwear
How great to actually get rid of it all in one go!
I never thought my body was ever gonna grow . . .
Out of this retro fashion!

I like to choose my clothes,
Of my own look, I want to be in charge.

Maybe the aliens wanted them for some Venus museum
Which wanted items back from space.
Oh how marvellous!
My underwear displayed in their glass case.

So that's why on their journey from the stars
The aliens stole my underpants.

Sandy Ni'Man (9)
Cringleford VA CE First & Middle School, Norwich

Space Pokèmon

P owerful sabres stalk on Pluto,
O n occasions a Farnut will attack,
K ing has nothing to do with Space Pokèmon.
È nter the world will mean death,
M onstrous Moroco is no match for a water sabre,
O nly capture them with the help of three,
N ever handle Space Pokèmon alone,

They live from the sun to the moon to Pluto!

Scott McCrum (9)
Cringleford VA CE First & Middle School, Norwich

My Auntie Rona

My auntie Rona
Is friendly, not a loner,
She likes hockey and football
She knows all the rules.
She sits in her armchair,
Doing her hair.
She loves chocolate digestives,
She dips them in her drink.
She likes eating bread
But it makes her go red.
She has a smile that brightens my day
It's warm, just like the sun's ray.
This is her way!

Debbie Stapleford (9)
Cringleford VA CE First & Middle School, Norwich

Tiger

Tiger prowling through the trees
Silence, then pounces, but no one sees.
It's fiery eyes glint in the moonlight,
Tiger sees a bright light.
Hunters with guns, tiger runs,
Leaping over logs and twigs
Bumping into wild pigs.
Tiger escapes, but only just.

Laura Doswell (9)
Cringleford VA CE First & Middle School, Norwich

School

S chool is fun, school is good,
   everybody goes in the neighbourhood.
C an't go in cos I'm really ill,
   need to take a sleeping pill.
H ope I'm soon going to get better,
   otherwise Mum will have to write a letter.
O ops, oh dear I've just been sick,
   got to go, quick, quick, quick.
O h no, oh dear, just lost my
   favourite teddy bear.
L ook I'm better now, I can go,
   see you later Tinky Winky and Po.

Emily Able (9)
Docking Primary School, Docking

Well It's NB Talking

Well it's NB talking
and NB's me.
I'm really funky
with my socks - jazzy.
Well I'm a popstar
with my Porsche car.
I'm going to the studio,
it's really funky as you know.
I'm driving around
with my windows down.
With my music on,
Oh look, I'm gone!

Nikki Brennan (10)
Docking Primary School, Docking

Pony

I have a pony in my garden
His favourite food is grass
When it's hot he rolls around
In the mud and it makes him brown.

I have a pony in my garden
He likes to brush his teeth
He opens his mouth and rubs his gums
On the long green grass.

I have a pony in my garden
He moves the hay with his feet
Then he eats and eats
And eats and eats . . .

Liam Craig (10)
Docking Primary School, Docking

Water

W hales are big fish, some say
A ll the fish swim round all day
T aps splash out
E veryone shout
R ain, hip hip hooray.

Alice Dean (9)
Docking Primary School, Docking

Rocking Docking

When Mum said, 'We're all moving house,'
I just sat moping, as quiet as a mouse.

Then she told me we're moving to Docking
And that's the village that's really rocking.

Now I've settled into school
All the teachers are really cool.

Mr Baldwin is who teaches me
And I'm just as happy as can be.

There is a really good fish and chip bar
We walk there, it's not too far.

I feed all the ducks on the village pond,
A white fluffy duck of which I'm very fond.

Over the road is a super park,
We can play, dogs can bark.

Don't forget the local Spar
If feeling lazy, we go in the car.

So moving to Docking hasn't been that bad
In fact, what a lot of fun I've had!

Holly Doyle (9)
Docking Primary School, Docking

Friends

Friends are fun, they play with us
Playing games, skipping with us.
They make us happy when we are sad,
They cheer us up and make us glad.

They tell us jokes that make me happy,
Playing funny games that make me laugh,
Time to go, time for bed
Cuddle with my smiley ted.

Wait till the next day,
See my friends and play again.

Danielle Durrant (9)
Docking Primary School, Docking

Cricket

C rack go the bats
R uns are the main thing in cricket
I ntelligent are the bowlers
C lear skies are the best for cricket
K eep it up team
E xcellent playing today team
T he test is over today.

Stephen English (10)
Docking Primary School, Docking

I Saw A Ship

I saw a ship a-sailing,
A-sailing on the sea,
I saw a man a-waving,
A-waving just at me.

I saw a lovely maiden,
A-skipping towards me,
Her hair was long and golden
As she ran along the quay.

The maid was searching for someone,
A sailor, keen and tall.
I think that she was searching for
That handsome sailor - Paul.

(Happy ending)
I saw a ship a-sailing
A-sailing to the quay,
Who will Paul come back to?
The lovely maiden or me.

(Sad ending)
I saw a ship a-sinking,
A-sinking on the sea,
Paul won't be coming back now
To the lovely maiden, me!

Poppy Everitt (10)
Docking Primary School, Docking

Cheeky Monkey

I went to the zoo
What did I see?
A cheeky monkey,
Lookin' at me.

I was reading the paper,
One sunny morning.
Drinking my tea
Then I was yawning.

I read a short piece,
About an ape - lost.
If you find it
You get some dosh.

Later that day
Saw a monkey called Dawn.
She was in my garden,
Cutting the lawn.

Then off the washing line,
She took my mum's bra,
She fastened it on
And strolled to Dad's car.

She started running
To our local zoo,
We all started cheering,
E'en me and you!

Jessica Freeland (10)
Docking Primary School, Docking

My New Puppy

I have a new puppy,
He rolls on his tummy,
He jumps up and down
And thinks meal times are yummy.

He chases a ball,
And bends it like Beckham,
If he played against France,
I know he would wreck 'em.

I love him to bits,
And I'm one lucky gal.
My puppy's the best
He's my friend, he's my pal.

Rebecca Gibbs (10)
Docking Primary School, Docking

Space

Up in space I float around,
It feels like there's just no sound.
When I fly out and about,
I'm really calm - there is no doubt.
When I come down to land,
I look at the stars from where I stand.

Joshua Howard (10)
Docking Primary School, Docking

Andrew's Innings

Lancashire chose to bat,
Andrew comes out with a hat.
Surrey bowled the opening ball,
And the bowler's very tall.

But Andrew hit it for a six,
It hit a child eating a Twix.
Andrew hit it for a four
And another! What a bore!

Andrew hit a single next,
A boy in the crowd received a text.
Andrew turned to look about
Oh no, Andrew Flintoft's out!

Callum Howell (10)
Docking Primary School, Docking

Football

I'm football crazy,
I'm really lazy.
I'm football mad
So's my dad.

Norwich City are the best,
From the cheers I must rest.
Aston Villa are so poor,
Aston Villa, still on tour.

Norwich City in a match,
But they've hit a rough patch.
Huckerby's almost scored,
But I'm totally bored.

Zoe Jenkins (10)
Docking Primary School, Docking

I'm Footie Crazy!

I'm footie crazy
I'm a Chelsea lad,
The best team in London
In fact, in the land.

Petr Cech in goal,
Wayne Bridge at left back.
Portuguese star Ferrera
Never pulls a hack.

John Terry and Gallas,
They're great fullbacks
Lampard and Makelele,
Centre of midfield.

Joe Cole on left wing,
He's a hero.
Tiago on right wing,
He's really on the go.

Eidur Gudjohnson
And Mutu,
Top strikers in Europe,
They'll try anything for you.

Alistair Kissock (9)
Docking Primary School, Docking

Football Crazy

I'm football crazy
I'm a West Ham lad.
If we don't win The Championship,
I'm gonna go mentally mad.

We're having a hard time,
We're really having it bad,
We have sold our best players
We've ever, ever had.

We have lost to Wigan
And at home,
What are we gonna do -
We need Henry on loan?

Teddy Sheringham
Is really on goal,
Even though he's 38
He's made the team whole.

Jack Murphy (10)
Docking Primary School, Docking

I Am Lonely

In my room, sitting on my chair
All I can hear is the whistling air,
I wish I had some caring friends
That's my wish, that's what God sends.
I'm lonely in my room
I sit waiting for something, soon.
People look and stare at me,
I look back with love and glee.
I bang my head against the wall,
I need a friend, please hear my call,
I hear children shouting out my name.
I go out, they've just made up a game.
I go to school, quiet as a mouse
Someone's invited me round to their house.
I think I've made a nice new friend,
I've got to go, can't tell you the end!

Rachel Ollive (10)
Docking Primary School, Docking

Olympic Games In Athens

Matthew Pinsent does the rowing,
While old granny at home does the sewing.
Matthew Pinsent wins the gold
While old granny's house gets all cold.

While Dean Macey does the Decathlon,
Paula Radcliffe does the marathon.
Deano Macey comes in fourth place
Paula Radcliffe loses her pace.

But old Great Britain tried her best,
And old Steve Backley needs a rest.
The Great Britain side are happy and proud,
They go back home and see their crowd.

Matthew Austin (9)
Docking Primary School, Docking

Max

There's a dog called Max
He sits on my lap
Then he goes to sleep
When he wakes up, I gave him some food

I take him out to play with his favourite ball
'Fetch' is his quickest game of all
At all the other games, he's slow
And when it turns dark, we go in.

Jessica Paget (10)
Docking Primary School, Docking

Dolly

It's Holly talking, and Holly's me,
My teddy's called Dolly and she's sitting next to me.
She's brown, soft and cuddly, her ears half chewed
because of me when I'm scared.
I hug her tight to make sure she's there all the time,
but when I'm happy I hold her hand and smother her with kisses
before I do ten handstands.
Everyday at half-past six, Dolly and me sit down to eat a Twix,
After that we go to the shop to buy a box of Haribo mix.
I'm in the bath, it's getting late
I must get out, I have a programme to tape
I'm out of the bath, my programme's taped,
Dolly and me are going to make a sponge cake
So I'll see you another day.

Sinead Ramshaw (10)
Docking Primary School, Docking

My Little Pony

I have a pony in my garden
she smiles when I give her food at 9.02.

I have a pony in my garden
when she's hot she runs and rolls
around in the mud to make her cold.

I have a pony in my garden,
she loves to go jumping in the field,
my mum is buying for you and me.

I have a pony in my garden,
we love to go jumping and racing
in the fields to win lots of rosettes.

I have a pony in my garden
she goes to bed at 10.53,
with lots of hay and snoozes until 7.45.

Zara Springford (10)
Docking Primary School, Docking

Acrostic

S plashing around all day,
W ater spilling over the side.
I can swim a mile,
M y mum watches me splish-sploshing around.
M oaning at my friend for pushing me in.
I turn around and swim off.
N oisy waves crashing down,
G oing to do a mile.

Lucy Vergerson (10)
Docking Primary School, Docking

Quad Bike Racing

They're at the start line
There are a few bets on number 15
Off they go, round the first corner just as I expected,
15 in front.
They come to the river - it's a strong current today
Are they going to make it?
Number 3 slips on a rock, oh no he's going too far down.
Will he be able to get back in the race?
He's out of here.
15's in front, 14 behind.
What's this? 15 is stuck in the mud,
14 gets through, 15 gets going again.
They're at the hill now.
10 skids but gets back control.
The next part is tricky - they have to dodge rocks
While going downhill across a stream and on dirt in the woodland
8's in front now, 15 is catching up,
Oh no, 8 has hit a tree!
Surely he's seeing birds go round his head!
They're out of the wood now, on the road, the finish is ahead
1st number 15, 2nd number 14 and 3rd number 10.

Sam Yelland (10)
Docking Primary School, Docking

Monkeys

M onkeys always prance around
O ver and over again
N ever are they sensible
K ind, but silly
E arth, not born
Y ou really ought to know

B ananas are what they eat
U sually all the time!
S ometimes they climb
I n trees or on the ground
N ever make friends with a monkey
E ven if they are sensible
S ometimes all we could do with monkeys doing is to . . .
S leep, sleep, *sleep!*

Charlotte Greenland (10)
Lake View Primary School, Mansfield

Night

A creak on the stairs,
Many shadows await you,
The curse of the dark.

A blindfold of mist,
The darkness swirls around you,
The thickness of black.

The ghosts are all up,
The witch is at her cauldron.
The vampires lurk.

The wind starts to blow,
Trees start to sway violently,
The hedge's leaves fall.

Matthew Northey (10)
Lake View Primary School, Mansfield

.

A Winter's Night

Looking through the window
Footprints in the snow
Watching children playing
Laughing as they go

Frost upon the glass
Glistens in the light
Stars shining brightly
On this winter's night

Gazing at the snowflakes
Falling from the sky
Snuggled up all cosy
Comfy, warm and dry.

Lindsey Peggs (10)
Lake View Primary School, Mansfield

The Haunted House

The ghost of the house
lights up the night sky
when people enter, they swell up and die.

When they enter, they face a trap
they fall on the floor, as the floor snaps.
As they fall, they will see the stars' gloom
through the wall cracks,
as they fall to their *doom*.

Luke Williams (10)
Lake View Primary School, Mansfield

The Sun

S hining brightly
U mbrellas not needed
N ice and warm.

Linzi Higgins (10)
Lake View Primary School, Mansfield

Night

N ight is sometimes friendly, sometimes harsh,
I t carries lots of secrets, secrets of the dark.
G oes on and on, it never stops.
H ow night is so dark, thick and overruling
T error struck in every heart.

Luke Bryant (11)
Lake View Primary School, Mansfield

Autumn

Flowers sway in the cold night air,
The trees around are bare.
Although the blossom season has gone,
The colour of the flowers in our mind goes on.
Now we start to wear gloves and hats
And cats curl up on their comfy mats
The wind picks up and flies up high
And waves the girls' and boys' ties.
Leaves flying everywhere
And little children stare
Coats are being
Fastened tight.
And down the
Street, autumn
Lights.

Emily Plastow
Lake View Primary School, Mansfield

Lions

Lions howling, lions prowling,
Waiting for the night to come.
Then they leave the darkness of the cave,
And into the silvery moonlight.
One glance of the lions,
The animals of the jungle run in fear,
And the little one's shed a tear.
When some of the animals fail their mission.

The lions return to their cave,
To eat the hunted meal.
Then howling, prowling,
Waiting for the night to come.

Dean Kennedy (10)
Lake View Primary School, Mansfield

Travelling

Music moving slowly through the air,
People stop and listen,
But there's nowhere to stare.

Moving from place to place,
Going everywhere,
At a certain pace.

Going fast or slow,
Loud or quiet,
Flying very low.

Listen with your ears,
Stare with your eyes,
And you will get a certain surprise!

Music!

Briony Dove (10)
Lake View Primary School, Mansfield

Jungle

J aguars are black, growling,
U nder the trees where
N utty gorillas hang.
G orillas are big and strong.
L ions are good at hunting.
E lephants are big and noisy.

Ryan Alsop (10)
Lake View Primary School, Mansfield

Where Am I?

Where am I? Worm world.
'Where am I?' monkeys yelled.
Where am I? Elephant earth.
Where am I? Land of Smurfs.
Where am I? Weirdo way.
Where am I? Crazy day.
Tell me where I am?

Elliott Phillips (8)
Our Lady Of Lourdes RC Primary School, Leigh-on-Sea

Christmas, Sight, Sense And Smell

We're going away to a sight which is
Nazareth, Nazareth, Nazareth, Nazareth.
We're going away to Nazareth
To find a baby king.

We're going to see him in a stable, in a stable,
We're going to see him in a stable
And find three wise men.

In the stable it smells of hay, smells of hay,
Smells of hay, in the stable it smells of hay
But Mary doesn't mind.

Mary calls the baby Jesus, Jesus, Jesus,
Mary calls the baby Jesus,
That's a nice name.

He's been born to spread the love,
Spread the love, spread the love,
He's been born to spread the word
And spread all the peace.

Kirsty Hickey (8)
Our Lady Of Lourdes RC Primary School, Leigh-on-Sea

Mum

She's nice, funny, silly,
And I love her so.
Sometimes she's horrible and scary.
My mum's tall, wears glasses,
Is pretty with browny-red hair
Which is short and curly.
Anything I want, she always says, 'No!'
But I still love her so!

Beth Norman (10)
St Augustine's Junior School, Worksop

The Supply Teacher

I walked into the classroom
To a deafening din,
And all of a sudden,
The teacher walked in.

I noticed she was different
To our normal one,
She waved a magic stick over a child,
Then he was gone.

With her spiky purple hair,
Glass eye and snotty nose,
She had flexing pink ears
And really scabby toes.

My friend began to whisper to me,
She turned him into a frog,
Then she took hold of him
And flushed him down the bog.

There was a loud bang
As the principal ran in,
The two began to have a fight,
He kept boxing her on the chin.

The principal won that fight,
Then he made a brand new rule,
'No more magic teachers!' he cried,
That was the most brilliant day at school.

Lewis Pettinger (10)
St Augustine's Junior School, Worksop

Stepdad

Stepdad, oh I love you so.
Anything I want, he never says no.
His big belly wobbles when he laughs so,
His impressions tickle you from head to toe.
His stubble is tickly,
His toes so smelly,
And when he trumps, you don't want to know.
But he loves me and I love him.
Stepdad, oh I love you so!

Emma Dent/Jackson (10)
St Augustine's Junior School, Worksop

Fat

Sugar, sugar, chips, chips,
Ready salted flavour crisps.
You're only fat because you're slacking,
Like my mum, she's always nagging.
Put yourself into shape,
And put on a serious face,
Do it, lose stones!
No, don't eat a jam scone!
Come on now, be serious,
I'm getting furious!
Lose some weight,
You will look great,
Or perhaps not!

Georgina Bagnall (10)
St Augustine's Junior School, Worksop

My Scribble

My pencil drew
Up, down, round and round,
My scribble could be . . .

A number one hit,
Filling all the shops,
Everyone loves it!

Or a piece of art,
In every gallery,
Everyone loves it!

Maybe a best selling novel,
No one can put it down,
Everyone loves it!

So if you're bored
With nothing to do,
Just draw your own scribble,
Have fun too!

Carrie-Ann Taylor (10)
St Augustine's Junior School, Worksop

When I Am On My Own

If it wasn't for my mum,
I would not eat things that are good for me,
Like carrots, swede and all my greens.
I would eat crisps, crisps and more crisps.

Crisps are good in one way,
Crisps are bad in another,
They're full of fat and bad for you,
But they taste so nice it's just not true!

If it wasn't for my grandma,
I would not know how to bake.
The things we bake taste great,
And sometimes we bake chocolate cake.

If it wasn't for my dad,
I would play loud music, wear false nails
And go out late with my mates.
If it wasn't for my dad, I would do everything he hates.

If it wasn't for my mum,
I am sure I would have lots of fun!

Wait one minute . . .

On my own sounds good,
But who would be my bestest mates then?

Sarah Cliffe (10)
St Augustine's Junior School, Worksop

The Journey

Long, long journeys, so boring,
Mum's snoring,
I'm drawing,
My sister's yawning,
It's so, so boring.
The streets fly by,
I'd rather eat apple pie
Than sit in the car
And watch the world zooming by.

Kate Knowles (10)
St Martin at Shouldham CE VA Primary School, King's Lynn

Dog

I wish I had a dog,
A dog that could
Clamp his jaws tight,
Bark like fierce wind,
Jump like a kangaroo,
Fetch a big stick,
Run like a car,
Play chase with me,
And that is what
I would like.

Dale Bettridge (9)
St Martin at Shouldham CE VA Primary School, King's Lynn

Holiday Race

One, two and three, we're ready to go.
It's holiday time, let's rock and roll!
Mum's in the back, Dad's at the wheel,
The sun's on my face, I love how warm it feels!

One, two and three, we're all in the car,
We're way ahead now, winning by far!
I'm all set to go, so let's rock and roll,
Oh no! What is this? Mum's been sick in a bowl!

One, two and three, we're catching up now,
Dad's whizzing away
Down the long motorway.
I can't believe it! We've won the race!
We've arrived without being sick at the holiday place!

Anna Blakie (10)
St Martin at Shouldham CE VA Primary School, King's Lynn

Rugby

Oval ball,
Real tall,
A kick over the post,
A kick to the coast,
A team real mean,
A team really keen,
Play on the pitch,
Be fantastically fit,
Rugby.

Oliver Ware (10)
St Martin at Shouldham CE VA Primary School, King's Lynn

Golf Ball

G oing
O ut of my mind
L earning this
F un game.

B ack of the hole
A ll the shots pin eye
L ob over the bunker
L eaving the course 2 under par.

Charlie Perkins (10)
St Martin at Shouldham CE VA Primary School, King's Lynn

Froggy Dog

There once was a frog
Who thought he was a dog
And once his dream came true
His leg went up
Like a mucky pup
And he had a tiddly due!

George Chapman (10)
St Martin at Shouldham CE VA Primary School, King's Lynn

A Drunk Man From Lancaster

There was a man from Lancaster
He was a beer drinking master,
He got so very drunk
His mother was sunk,
Oh, that drunk man from Lancaster.

Rory Blake (9)
St Martin at Shouldham CE VA Primary School, King's Lynn

A Chocolate Advertisement

It's either bright or creamy white,
It could be Mars
Or other chocolate bars.
The soft milk,
It is so silk,
Some have a hint
Of some mint.
It may be unhealthy,
But it makes you feel wealthy.
It makes you think, *wow!*
So try it - now!

Liam Holbeche-Smith (9)
St Martin at Shouldham CE VA Primary School, King's Lynn

The Dog From China

There was an old dog from China,
He went to a kitchen diner.
He ate a big burger,
And couldn't go further,
That stuffed old dog from China.

Oliver Johnson (9)
St Martin at Shouldham CE VA Primary School, King's Lynn

A Young Gymnast

There was a young gymnast called Grace,
Whose backflips were really quite ace!
One day doing handstands
In her own school bandstand,
She fell down on her face!

Katherine Blakie (10)
St Martin at Shouldham CE VA Primary School, King's Lynn

Kayaking

K ayaking down a stream,
A round the bends,
Y ahoo through the rapids,
A nd down the waterfall.
K eeping away from the banks,
I mpossible to turn,
N ot knowing how to stop,
G ood, I hit the bank!

Lewis Findull (10)
St Martin at Shouldham CE VA Primary School, King's Lynn

Waves

The coastguard watches in the mist
As the waves crash on the big cliffs,
So he sees the big light,
And has a big fright,
That coastguard who watches the mist.

Morgan Massurit (9)
St Martin at Shouldham CE VA Primary School, King's Lynn

Magic

Witches and wizards and coal-black cats,
Potions and broomsticks, and flying bats,
Hats and cloaks, with moons and stars,
Witches use broomsticks and humans use cars.

Kayley Stabler (9)
St Martin at Shouldham CE VA Primary School, King's Lynn

Light

The light is going
Into night,
So early, so right,
Streetlight shadow and flicking up starlight,
Everybody is in a fright,
So don't come out tonight . . .

Maisie Silverman (10)
St Martin at Shouldham CE VA Primary School, King's Lynn

The Old Lady

There was an old lady who wore a shawl,
She had a husband whose name was Paul.
She looked around town all day
Trying to book a holiday.
She saw an ad that said 'Spain',
But she was not so keen on the plane.
So she stayed at home
Eating an ice cream cone.

Jasmine Haskett (10)
St Martin at Shouldham CE VA Primary School, King's Lynn

Lotty The Dog

Lotty is a dog,
She likes a belly rub.
She came in and bit her bone.
She likes to run and play every day.

Daniella Bottone (9)
St Martin at Shouldham CE VA Primary School, King's Lynn

The Football Ticket

Football is my favourite sport,
More than any other sort.
I love to shoot at goal,
Not putting in a hole.
I'd rather pass and shoot
And wear my football boots.
No not tennis, no not cricket,
I'd rather buy my football ticket.

Calum Wilson (11)
St Martin at Shouldham CE VA Primary School, King's Lynn

Hose

The hose can squeeze
Water to a silver rod
That digs hard holes in the mud.

Or, muzzled tighter by the nozzle,
Can rain chilled diamond chains
Across the yard.

Or fanned out fine,
Can hang a silk rainbow halo
Over soft fog.

Greg Mitchell (10)
St Martin at Shouldham CE VA Primary School, King's Lynn

Black Widow

I'm in love with a black widow,
Yes, the most poisonous spider in the world.
She makes me feel warm,
The glamour she has,
Her silky web shines in the moonlight.

Ben Stanhope (11)
Townley School, Christchurch

I Am The One

I am the engine that starts the keys,
I am the door that opens the hand,
I am the carpet that cleans the Hoover,
I am the food that cooks the oven,
I am the wood that cuts the saw,
I am the car that cleans the jet wash.

Aaron Whittaker (10)
Townley School, Christchurch

My Dog

My favourite animal is a dog.
When it's night-time he is as dark as a log.
In the morning he is ready for a jog.
When we tell him off he gets in a strop,
Then he sobs all day
Until he gets to play,
And then he is happy again.

Daniel Rushton (10)
Townley School, Christchurch

Dancing Dolphins

Dolly the dolphin
Dancing in the waves,
Having an adventure,
All the time to play.

Performance and action,
Diving in the deep,
She can never sleep,
It's a memory I'll keep.

I'm starting to fall asleep,
So she swims off to eat.
She swims to a certain beat,
Her skin is like a sheet,
And now I'm asleep.

Emily Chisholm (10)
Townley School, Christchurch

That Squirrel!

That squirrel has some nuts,
That squirrel is climbing a tree,
That squirrel is storing the nuts,
That squirrel flees away,
That squirrel drops from the air,
That squirrel runs up to me,
That squirrel glares up at me,
Then that squirrel runs away.

Alex Andrews (10)
Townley School, Christchurch

If I Was

If I was a sailor,
I'd sail the sea
And look at all the countries,
And stay there maybe.
If I was a wasp,
I'd buzz all around.
If I was an ant,
I'd crawl on the ground.
If I was a wrestler,
I'd beat all of them.
I'd beat them; I'd beat them,
And I'd beat them again!

Ollie Haylock (10)
Townley School, Christchurch

The Harvest Festival

I am the swedes, crispy and crunchy,
I am the potatoes cut for chips,
I am the seeds in the melon,
I am the juice in the blackcurrant,
And I am the layers of an onion.

Steven Leeman (10)
Townley School, Christchurch

Blu-tack

Blu-tack it's sticky, it's blue,
It's Blu-tack!
You can make a cat or a hat or a mat or a splat,
Blu-tack it's sticky, it's blue,
It's Blu-tack!
It's fiddly, it's roly, it's lots of fun,
Blu-tack, the fun has just begun.

Georgina Clifford (10)
Townley School, Christchurch

Zara The Dog

Zara was so sweet,
She used to lick my feet.

She was brown and black,
She had a lovely soft back.

Zara was so old,
And her nose was so cold.

When Zara died,
I cried and cried.

Ryan Tominey (10)
Townley School, Christchurch

The Moon And The Stars

It is a full moon tonight,
I love the moon, it's always lovely and bright.
It keeps an eye on me every night.

The stars are out tonight,
They are lovely and bright.
The stars are like little flashing lights.

I love the moon and the stars.
I will see you another night.

Becca Jackson (10)
Townley School, Christchurch

Winter Is Here

It's a cold, damp night, winter must be here.
I woke up in the morning, *surprise*, snow had appeared.
The sunlight beamed from the snow straight into the eye,
The twinkling snow laying on the ground without a sound.
It's bouncing off the window, pattering on the door,
Now I know that winter is here.

Ellie Jackson (10)
Townley School, Christchurch

Rugby Crazy!

Rugby crazy, ice cream mad,
I've been playing rugby
Since I was a lad.

Rugby crazy, Jonny's the man,
He won the World Cup
And I'm his biggest fan.

Rugby crazy, rugby mad,
All my family play it
Cos we're all rugby mad!

Damien Campbell Warby (10)
Townley School, Christchurch

My Little Rabbit

There was a little rabbit
Who often visited me,
We'd play for hours and hours
Until he went home for tea.

There was a little rabbit
Who often visited me,
We'd climb all the mountains
And sail all the seas.

There was a little rabbit
Who often visited me,
We found a treasure chest one day
With a magic key.

There was a little rabbit
Who often visited me,
We opened up the chest
But there was nothing we could see.

There was a little rabbit,
Who often visited me,
We'd play for hours and hours
Until he went home for tea.

Chantelle Coxall (10)
Townley School, Christchurch

Ode To A Cheese Roll

Oh glorious, amazing cheese roll,
How your flavour makes my taste buds explode!
I look forward to lunchtime because of you.
The way that I wolf down half of your cheesy delights,
Whilst the other half stares up at me from your container.
How wonderfully your bite-sized chunks pop into my mouth with ease.
Your addictive cheesy filling in my mouth
As my stomach longs for more.
The fabulous smell that reaches my nostrils
As I open the lid of the Tupperware!
I inhale the cheesy whiff of pure, organic,
Old English farmhouse cheddar . . .
So mature!
Oh glorious, admirable cheese roll,
What would I do without you?

Ernest Hill (10)
Wheatfields Junior School, St Albans

My Feet

My arch is as bumpy as a country road,
The skin between my toes is as floppy as a Labrador's ear,
The toenail is like a snail's shell.
My veins are a maze of rivers and streams,
The bone at the back of my heel is like an Egyptian spear.
My ankle is like a mountain standing proud in the creamy sky.
The ball of my foot is orange-soft at the bottom,
But apple-hard at the top.

Tom Girdlestone (10)
Wheatfields Junior School, St Albans

Autumn Leaves

Leaves are fluttering from the tops of the trees,
swooping gently to join the rest of their family.
Silky as spiders' webs,
Fluffy as clouds,
Rough as curtains,
Smooth as babies' hands,
Orange as a sunset,
Brown as mud,
Yellow as the sun,
Red as ripe strawberries.
Darkening over time . . .
Dying. Slowly but surely.
Being stamped and stomped on!
Lying on the ground.
Crunching, scrunching . . . like sandpaper.
Starting to crumble into tiny pieces like a jigsaw puzzle.

Francesca Knight (9)
Wheatfields Junior School, St Albans

Orange

A sweet, juicy orange sitting in the fruit bowl.
The sunset, with its huge glow bleeding into the horizon.
Fallen leaves in autumn, so beautiful to see.
Marigolds brightening the garden.
A bonfire crackling with ashes in the evening.
A mixture of spikes which would prick your finger whilst they sparkled.
The end of the day, time to rest.

James Riding (8)
Wheatfields Junior School, St Albans

My Foot

My sole is as squishy as a cooked mushroom,
My little toe like a baby slug.
The toenails are like a turtle's shell.
When I wiggle my toes, I see the bones move.
The skin on my heel is as tough and rough as rhino skin.
The top of my foot is table-top smooth,
With patterns and markings like the bark on a tree
And a barren landscape on the sole of my foot.

Raveena Virdee (10)
Wheatfields Junior School, St Albans

Blackberries

I see this blackberry
Shining in the sun,
Purple-black as the night sky,
Squidgy and bumpy
With tiny bristles.

I just can't reach it,
I'm shivering with excitement.
Ooh! The smell makes me dribble.
My hand twists and turns,
I'm just trying to grab that glorious blackberry.

I'm reaching so far . . .
Just in front of me
My shiny jewel stone.
I pluck so violently that I nearly fall over.
I drop it in my mouth,
I feel so vibrant.
Yummm!

Lydia Spooner (9)
Wheatfields Junior School, St Albans

Blackberry

I push the thorny branch aside,
My hand, shivering with anticipation,
Gets poked and prodded by knife-sharp thorns.
Reaching for the shiny, black-armoured berry,
I can imagine the taste . . .
Ripe, juicy, sweet as sugar.
I finally get my hands on that beautiful ripe jewel.
I pluck my prize off the mud-brown branch,
It's as soft as white tissue
As it touches my lips.

Brent McCormick (10)
Wheatfields Junior School, St Albans

Bubbles

Bubbles flitter around the room,
I see a rainbow of colours in them.
They catch my eye when they fly past me,
Gliding out as magical spheres,
Spinning gracefully in the air,
Drifting down and popping quietly.
They move like a fluttery butterfly with invisible wings.
They flutter past me, like they are jogging to get fit.
They remind me of a baby's head bobbing up and down.
They swim past me like fish.

Kate Upton (8)
Wheatfields Junior School, St Albans

Autumn Leaves

Autumn leaves floating gently,
Colourful as ever.
Street lamp orange,
Apple red.
Feeling like soft, leathery snakeskin.
Drifting down in their distinctive shapes,
Zigzaggy,
Curly,
Twisty and swirly.
When they hit the ground the wind blows them round,
Suddenly they alter direction.
Weeks pass . . .
They gradually change -
Start to crumble,
And their beautiful blood-reds turn to dull browns.

Jack Caddy (9)
Wheatfields Junior School, St Albans

Doughnut

I pick the doughnut from the box,
Glistening in the light
With its toffee-brown surface,
Holding the taste in . . .
I take a bite!
As my teeth sink into the spongy innards,
The sugar tickles my tongue.
Savouring it all
I swallow,
And I'm left with the feeling of contentment.

Richard Breislin (10)
Wheatfields Junior School, St Albans

Conkers

The spiky shell of a conker
Just ready to be opened,
Waiting . . .
In the crunchy cushion of leaves,
Crack!
It opens.
The shiny chestnut brown
Glimmering like moonlight in the dark brown curtain of the sky.
It feels like a special stone
Wrapped in velvet,
Smells like polished shoes.
The tops feel rough,
Like bark on a tree.
The swirls on a conker look like patterns on a snail shell.
It feels table-top smooth.
Oh no! A squashed conker!
The inside looks like mushy cheese-coloured peas,
And it feels as hard as wood.
The conker drops out of my hand,
It doesn't want me anymore,
So I leave it once again in the soft cushion
Of bright gold, ruby-red, crunchy brown leaves.

Holly Winfield (8)
Wheatfields Junior School, St Albans

Doughnuts

Delicious doughnuts,
They're all squidgy and sticky
On my fingertips and around my mouth.
Sometimes they've got sugar on,
Crumbly crystals sparkling in the light.
A rim of pale custard all the way around.
A spongy feeling,
Like Mum's hair in the morning.
Doughnuts! Oh doughnuts!
Giving me the urge to bite.
One bite . . .
First bite . . .
Great!
Second bite . . . even better!
The blood-red jam bulging out of the centre.
So sweet and gorgeous.
Oh marvellous doughnuts,
How could I ever live without you?

Paige Young (10)
Wheatfields Junior School, St Albans

Bubbles

Bubbles glisten as they move,
Suddenly, silently disappearing.
Rainbow colours appear on their delicate transparent skins.
They glide through the air like glass balls spinning.
I catch them,
They sit there for a few seconds . . .
Then they disappear,
Leaving a droplet of sticky, gooey liquid in the palm of my hands.

Larissa Begg (8)
Wheatfields Junior School, St Albans

Conker

Swaying in the wind,
A conker in its shell.
A small porcupine hanging by its tail.
It unwraps itself, falling like a diver,
Cutting through the air,
Gripping the ground with its spiky shell.
Half of the shell breaks and opens,
A conker steps out of its bed
Shining in the light of the sun.
It crawls amongst the endless carpet of leaves
And sits on the autumn floor
Waiting to be found.

Jonathan Chambers (9)
Wheatfields Junior School, St Albans

Ode To Jaffa Cakes

Oh marvellously glorious Jaffa Cake,
Your perfumey, chocolatey smell brightens my day.
An exquisite top layer of delightfully bitter chocolate
Warms me with joy.
Your fabulous tangy centre,
Your sticky, smooth feel,
Your succulent orangey taste makes my tongue tickle with excitement.
Such an admirable bottom layer.
As my mouth reaches you I know the esteemed event is almost over.
That tremendous soggy, spongy texture gives me a reason to live.
Oh exceptional Jaffa Cake,
You are the most beautiful treat ever to appear on this Earth.
Oh honourable, noble, saintly, righteous, praiseworthy,
Celebrated, classic, holy Jaffa Cake . . .
You are simply divine!

Nicholas Gachowicz (11)
Wheatfields Junior School, St Albans

Gold

Gold treasure, solid and heavy.
The cuddle of my teddy, Security.
Autumn leaves as they whisper in the breeze.
The spirit of the sky.
Gold is the taste of the ends of the Earth.
The touch of my granny sewing a warm jumper for me,
Too lovely to let go of.
That's what gold is!

Joseph Crosby (8)
Wheatfields Junior School, St Albans